Man
in
School

Pitman Publishing

First published 1972

Sir Isaac Pitman and Sons Ltd
Pitman House, Parker Street, Kingsway, London WC2B 5PB
PO Box 46038, Portal Street, Nairobi, Kenya

Sir Isaac Pitman (Aust) Pty Ltd
Pitman House, 158 Bouverie Street, Carlton, Victoria 3053, Australia

Pitman Publishing Company SA Ltd
PO Box 11231, Johannesburg, South Africa

Pitman Publishing Corporation
6 East 43rd Street, New York, NY 10017, USA

Sir Isaac Pitman (Canada) Ltd
495 Wellington Street West, Toronto 135, Canada

The Copp Clark Publishing Company
517 Wellington Street West, Toronto 135, Canada

ISBN: 0 273 00016 0

Reproduced and printed by photolithography and bound in Great Britain
at The Pitman Press, Bath

G3372:11

STAFF
v
SCHOOL